WHAT ON EARTH IS A
CHUCKWALLA

EDWARD R. RICCIUTI

 A BLACKBIRCH PRESS BOOK

WOODBRIDGE, CONNECTICUT

Published by Blackbirch Press, Inc.
260 Amity Road
Woodbridge, CT 06525

©1994 Blackbirch Press, Inc.
First Edition

Printed in Hong Kong

10 9 8 7 6 5 4 3 2

Photo Credits

Cover, title page: ©Zig Leszczynski/Animals Animals.
Pages 4—5: ©George H.H. Huey/Animals Animals; pages 6—7: ©John Gerlach/Animals Animals; pages 8—9: ©E.R. Degginger/Animals Animals; page 11: ©Zig Leszczynski/Animals Animals; page 12: ©Dan Suzio/Photo Researchers, Inc; page 15: ©Mickey Gibson/Animals Animals; page16: ©Stepan J. Krasemann/Photo Researchers, Inc; pages 18—19: ©Miriam Austerman/Animals Animals; page 20: ©Zig Leszczynski/Animals Animals; pages 22—23: ©Tom McHugh/Photo Researchers, Inc.; page 25: ©Tom McHugh/Photo Researchers, Inc.; page 26: ©Zig Leszczynski/Animals Animals; page 28: ©Dan Suzio/Photo Researchers, Inc.

Library of Congress Cataloging-in-Publication Data
Ricciuti, Edward R.
What on earth is a chuckwalla? / by Edward R. Ricciuti. — 1st ed.
    p.   cm. — (What on earth series)
    Includes bibliographical references (p.   ) and index.
    ISBN 1-56711-089-4
    1. Chuckwalla—Juvenile literature.   [1. Chuckwalla.
2. Lizards.]   I. Title.   II. Series.
QL666.L25R53   1994
597.95—dc20

94-28248
CIP
AC

What does it look like?

Where does it live?

What does it eat?

How does it reproduce?

How does it survive?

TURN THESE PAGES AND FIND OUT!

A chuckwalla is a small, chubby animal with a large head and a puffy belly. Heavy folds of skin droop from its throat, neck, and shoulders. Its skin is rough and scaly and its long, thick tail drags along the ground as it moves slowly across the rocks and sand of its habitat.

A CHUCKWALLA IS A SCALY
CREATURE THAT LOOKS LIKE
A MINIATURE DINOSAUR.

A chuckwalla is a lizard. It belongs to a family of lizards called iguanids. There are lots of different kinds, or species, of iguanids—about 700 all together. Almost all of them live in North America, South America, and nearby islands.

Iguanids have two basic body shapes. Most iguanids that live in trees are flattened side to side. Iguanids that live on the ground, like the chuckwalla, have bodies that are flattened top to bottom. Because they are low to the ground, they are more difficult for enemies to see. Their shape also helps them to hide in rock crevices.

CHUCKWALLAS, LIKE MOST IGUANIDS THAT LIVE ON THE GROUND, HAVE LOW, FLAT BODIES.

The chuckwalla probably got its common name from Native Americans of the Shoshone tribes that lived in the southwestern desert areas of North America. The scientific name of the main species of chuckwalla is *Sauromalus obesus*.

Those are Greek and Latin terms that mean "fat, bad lizard." The chuckwalla certainly is fat. But, the only thing really "bad" about it is its looks. It is not very pretty. Some people say that the chuckwalla looks like a mini-dragon or a dinosaur.

THE CHUCKWALLA'S SCIENTIFIC NAME, WHICH MEANS "FAT, BAD LIZARD," REFERS TO ITS PUFFY BODY SHAPE.

The color of chuckwallas varies. Overall, adults are dark, even black. Most chuckwallas have yellow, red, or gray dots sprinkled on their backs. These colors grow brighter toward the rear of the body. Females often have gray and yellow cross bands, especially on their tails.

Chuckwallas are pudgy creatures, with big heads and pot bellies. A large one can be 1.5 feet (46 centimeters) long and weigh more than 3 pounds (1 kilogram). The tail of a chuckwalla is round and thick. Heavy folds of skin droop from a chuckwalla's throat, neck, and shoulders. In fact, its skin is so loose that it looks too large for the chuckwalla's fat body.

Many lizards have teeth set atop the bone in their jaws. Iguanids, however, are different. Their teeth grow in a groove on the inner side of their jawbones. When a tooth wears out or is lost, a new one replaces it.

MOST CHUCKWALLAS HAVE COLORED DOTS SPRINKLED ON THEIR BACKS. IN GENERAL, THE COLORS ON A CHUCKWALLA'S BODY GET BRIGHTER TOWARD THE TAIL.

CHUCKWALLAS REGULATE THEIR BODY TEMPERATURE BY SEEKING SUN WHEN THEY NEED TO WARM UP OR SHADE IF THE TEMPERATURE GETS TOO HOT.

Chuckwallas live in deserts. They especially like rocky places, with many boulders. They are found in southeastern California, southern Nevada and Utah, western Arizona, and northern Mexico. Chuckwallas also live on 22 islands in Mexico's Gulf of California. These island chuckwallas are the largest. Some of them are 2 feet (61 centimeters) long and are called "giant chuckwallas."

During the day, chuckwalla country can be very hot. At night, the air can be very cold. Like snakes and turtles, lizards are reptiles. A reptile's body cannot make its own heat the way yours can. In hot surroundings, a reptile's body heats up. In cold surroundings, it cools down.

If it is too hot, a chuckwalla may get into the nearest shade or crawl underground to keep from overheating. Temperatures below the desert's surface do not change as much as up above. So if the air temperature rises too high or drops too low, the chuckwalla may look for a hole and crawl into it.

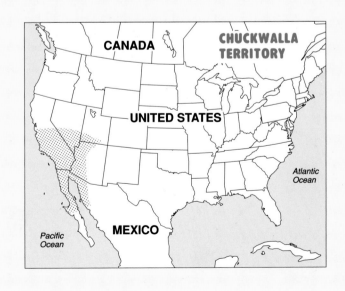

Despite its fierce appearance, the chuckwalla does not often bother other creatures. It eats only plants—leaves, fruits, and flowers.

For some reason, hungry chuckwallas are attracted to the color yellow. Their two favorite food plants, a prickly pear cactus and the creosote bush, both have yellow flowers.

Chuckwallas, like many other desert animals, feed mostly in the early morning and evening. During those times, it is neither too hot nor too cold. So instead of working to regulate its body temperature, the chuckwalla can concentrate on finding a meal. Then it eats slowly, only one bite at a time.

CHUCKWALLAS EAT ONLY LEAVES, FRUITS, AND FLOWERS FOUND IN NORTH AMERICA'S DESERT SOUTHWEST.

CHUCKWALLAS SHARE THEIR
DESERT HABITAT WITH MANY
OTHER ANIMALS. HERE, A
CHUCKWALLA (LEFT) STANDS
NEXT TO A COLLARED LIZARD
(RIGHT).

Many other animals share the desert with the chuckwalla. They include other reptiles, such as spiny lizards, zebra-tailed lizards, horned lizards, rattlesnakes, coral snakes, western whip snakes, and desert tortoises.

Several kinds of hawks also live in chuckwalla country. In fact, many birds live there. Turkey vultures soar through the air. Elf owls perch on cacti. Quail and roadrunners scurry over the ground.

The desert is also the home of several mammals. Larger types include desert bighorn sheep, mule deer, and pronghorns. Predators—hunters—include the coyote, gray fox, kit fox, and bobcat. Rodents are especially numerous. Some common kinds are ground squirrels, kangaroo rats, pack rats, and pocket mice.

CHUCKWALLAS ARE MAINLY HUNTED
AND KILLED BY HAWKS AND OTHER
LARGE BIRDS.

The main predators of chuckwallas are mostly hawks. The red-tailed hawk, which is common in chuckwalla country, often eats reptiles. Ravens also feed on chuckwallas. Small chuckwallas may also be caught and eaten by roadrunners.

20

What On Earth
Is a
Chuckwalla?

CHUCKWALLAS CAN INFLATE THEIR BODIES WITH AIR AS A DEFENSE AGAINST ENEMIES. ONCE A CHUCKWALLA IS WEDGED IN BETWEEN SOME ROCKS, IT IS EXTREMELY HARD TO GET IT OUT.

When a chuckwalla is in danger, it creeps into a rock crevice. Once inside, it inhales air through its nostrils and gulps more air through its mouth. It uses its thick tongue to force the air down into its lungs. The chuckwalla can push 300 times more air into its lungs than when it breathes normally! As its lungs fill up with air, the chuckwalla's body swells, filling up its skin. Blown up, its body may be expanded by more than a half! When swollen, it becomes firmly wedged between the rocks. The chuckwalla's rough skin helps to hold it in place. Once a chuckwalla is wedged in, even a strong person may not be able to pull it out.

Chuckwallas must be well fed in order to mate and have young. During droughts, food plants are scarce and mating may not take place. When food is plentiful, chuckwallas mate during May and June. Large males stake out a territory with plants and boulders that attract females. The males that control the best territories mate with the most females.

A male will defend his territory against other males. Sometimes a male will bite and lash out with his tail. Usually, though, males try to bluff each other by looking fierce. In a bluff battle, a male may arch its back, lower and bob its head, and open its mouth. It may also puff out its throat with air and turn sideways to make itself look larger. When one male has had enough, or is scared, he retreats.

MALE CHUCKWALLAS STAKE OUT TERRITORIES WITH PLANTS AND ROCKS TO ATTRACT FEMALES DURING MATING SEASON.

Chuckwallas usually mate between the ages of 4 to 7 years. A male will use movements, such as bobbing its head, to attract females to mate. He may also nose the female with his snout. If the female is ready to mate, the male climbs on her back. Then he inserts sperm into her body. The sperm fertilizes her eggs. Once the eggs are fertilized, new organisms begin to develop.

When the female is ready to lay her eggs, she digs a burrow. It is about as long and wide as her body. At the far end of the burrow, she makes a large chamber. She turns around in the chamber with her head facing the burrow's entrance. Then she lays her eggs.

Most female chuckwallas lay between 6 to 13 eggs. However, some of the giants may lay more than 30. When the female finishes egg laying, she fills up the burrow, except for the chamber, and leaves. Secretions left behind by the female keep the burrow and eggs moist.

AFTER THEY HAVE MATED, FEMALES DEPOSIT THEIR EGGS IN A BURROW, WHERE THEY WILL EVENTUALLY HATCH.

AN ADULT CHUCKWALLA WATCHES OVER ONE OF ITS OFFSPRING. YOUNG
CHUCKWALLAS TYPICALLY HAVE STRIPES OR BANDS ON THEIR BODIES,
ESPECIALLY ON THEIR TAILS.

Chuckwalla eggs hatch in about three months. After hatching, the young dig their way to the outside world through the loose soil in the burrow. Some scientists think that the young chuckwallas take turns digging. When one is tired, another may take over.

Most newly hatched chuckwallas are about 2.5 inches (63 millimeters) long. Both male and female young have cross bands on their bodies and tails. Most male chuckwallas lose their bands as they grow older. Females often keep their cross bands, especially on their tails.

THE DELICATE BALANCE OF NATURE
IN THE CHUCKWALLA'S HABITAT IS
EASILY DISTURBED. HUMANS MUST
TAKE CARE TO PROTECT THESE
HABITATS SO CHUCKWALLAS AND
OTHER ANIMALS CAN SURVIVE.

The desert environment in which chuckwallas live is easily disturbed. Native plants of the desert have been destroyed—by off-road vehicles and other human activities—and do not grow back. Clearing land for construction is also damaging chuckwalla habitats. Without habitats, animals cannot survive.

Today, many people like to keep chuckwallas as pets. Some catch chuckwallas on their own. Others have bought them from pet stores. Many chuckwallas that are for sale have been taken from the wild. People have captured so many giant chuckwallas from the Gulf of California that they are now very rare. Scientists at the Arizona-Sonora Desert Museum in Tucson, Arizona, are breeding large numbers of giant chuckwallas. Even though they are still rare, chances are good this species will not become extinct. But it is only through the efforts of concerned scientists and conservationists that the giant chuckwalla is being helped. If chuckwallas are to survive in the future, humans must take care not to ruin the delicate balance of nature in the chuckwalla's world.

Glossary

burrow An underground nest or home.

egg Female sex cell.

extinct No longer in existence.

fertilization The union of sperm and egg that creates a new organism.

habitat The surroundings in which an organism lives, containing everything it needs to survive.

Iguanids The family of lizards to which the chuckwalla belongs.

predator An animal that hunts other animals for food.

scientific name A name for an organism that is the same all over the world. The scientific name for the chuckwalla is *Sauromalus obesus.*

sperm Male sex cell.

territory A specific area claimed by an animal or group of animals.

Further Reading

Bailey, Donna. *Lizards*. Morristown, NJ: Raintree
  Steck-Vaughn, 1992.

Baker, Lucy. *Life in the Deserts*. New York: Watts,
  1990.

Caitlin, Stephen. *Discovering Reptiles &
  Amphibians*. Mahwah, NJ: Troll, 1990.

Chinery, Michael. *Desert Animals*. New York:
  Random House, 1992.

Fagan, Elizabeth G. *Rand McNally Children's Atlas
  of World Wildlife*. Chicago: Rand McNally, 1993.

Few, Roger. *Macmillan Animal Encyclopedia for
  Children*. New York: Macmillan Child Group, 1991.

Johnson, Jinny. *Desert Wildlife*. New York: Readers
  Digest, 1993.

Losito, Linda. *Reptiles and Amphibians*. New York:
  Facts On File, 1989.

Ricciuti, Edward R. *Reptiles*. Woodbridge, CT:
  Blackbirch Press, 1993.

Richardson, Joy. *Reptiles*. New York: Franklin Watts,
  1993.

Smith, Trevor. *Amazing Lizards*. New York: Knopf
  Books for Young Readers, 1990.

Twist, Clint. *Deserts*. New York: Macmillan, 1991.

Index